When students encounter a new word, they may decode the word without understanding its meaning, or they may guess the meaning using context clues. However, students with morphological awareness have a powerful tool for decoding and making sense of unfamiliar words. For example, if students know the prefix *mis-*, they will pronounce it automatically and they will understand how the prefix modifies the meaning of the base word. And if the base word includes a familiar root, such as *nom* (meaning *name*), the meaning of the unfamiliar word *misnomer* is more easily understood.

According to researchers, by the end of high school, the average student knows 80,000 vocabulary words. Clearly, not all of them, not even a small percentage of them, were taught through explicit instruction. There are simply too many words and too little time. Giving students strategic tools to deepen their understanding of known words will help them unlock the meaning of new words. *Vocabulary Packets: Prefixes and Suffixes* makes the learning fun and playful.

Words are power. Prefixes and suffixes are power tools.

How to Use the Book

Vocabulary Packets: Prefixes and Suffixes covers 50+ prefixes and suffixes and 150+ words with affixes. Each unit provides practice with five affixes and related words over the course of four lessons.

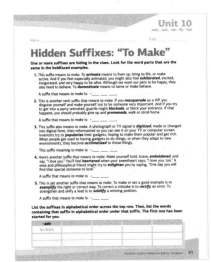

ACTIVITY 1

Hidden Prefixes/Hidden Suffixes: Students use clues from three examples of words with the affix to figure out the affix. Then students list the words for each affix alphabetically.

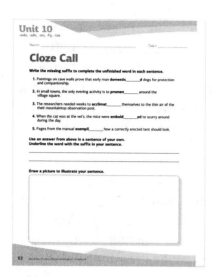

ACTIVITY 2

Cloze Call: Students supply the affix that completes the unfinished word in a context sentence. Then students select a word and write and illustrate a sentence for it.

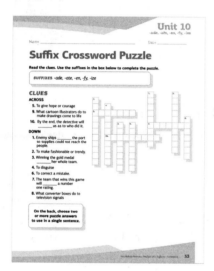

ACTIVITY 3

Crossword Puzzle: Students complete the crossword puzzle with words from the unit. They also compose a sentence using two or more of the answers.

ACTIVITY 4

Student-Made Word Cards: Students complete affix definitions and the definitions of the words from the unit. Challenge students to add other words with the affix from their general and content-area reading. There is space provided for additional words (see Teaching Tips for more on additional words). On the back of each card, students write a sentence and illustrate one word.

SCHOLASTIC

Vocabulary Packets

Prefixes & Suffixes

by Liane B. Onish

NEW YORK • TORONTO • LONDON • AUCKLAND • SYDNEY
MEXICO CITY • NEW DELHI • HONG KONG • BUENOS AIRES

Teaching *Resources*

Hi, Mom!

Edited by Sarah Longhi
Content editing by Eileen Judge
Cover design by Ka-Yeon Kim
Interior design by Brian LaRossa

ISBN-13: 978-0-545-19864-6
ISBN-10: 0-545-19864-X
Copyright © 2010 by Liane B. Onish.
All rights reserved. Published by Scholastic Inc.
Printed in the U.S.A.

1 2 3 4 5 6 7 8 9 10   40   16 15 14 13 12 11 10

Contents

Introduction

The goal of *Vocabulary Packets: Prefixes and Suffixes* is to introduce, reinforce, and provide practice with affixes. The activities are game-oriented to make learning fun. Students will have multiple encounters with each affix to reinforce learning so they can "own" their new knowledge. Over the course of a week, students will use clues to find affixes in interesting vocabulary words, complete cloze sentences, use words with prefixes and suffixes to complete crossword puzzles, and practice the words in review games. The rewards are the "aha!" moments as learners gain a deeper understanding of individual and related words and acquire powerful tools to unlock the meanings of new words.

What the Research Says

Words are the name of the game. The more words you know, the more words you can speak, read, and write. The key to the game is learning as many new words as possible. Morphological awareness—the ability to identify meaningful parts of words (morphemes), including prefixes, suffixes and root words—can help.

- ▶ Morphological awareness improves decoding accuracy and fluency (Nagy, 2005). Decoding accuracy and speed improves when students can process larger chunks of text quickly. When students are able to recognize morphemes in increasingly complex words, reading speed increases, and students are better able to make sense of new and complex words in context.

- ▶ For every word known by students who can make use of morphology and context, an estimated additional one to three words should also be understandable (Nagy & Anderson, 1984). **Students who know prefixes, suffixes, and roots can effectively double or triple their vocabularies!**

- ▶ Current research suggests that morphological awareness is the strongest consistent predictor of success for reading comprehension, reading vocabulary, and spelling.

- ▶ Morphological awareness impacts vocabulary growth (Nagy, 2005). Effective word-meaning instruction built on teaching key words, roots, and morphology results in stronger word attack and vocabulary skills.

- ▶ Research shows that morphological awareness contributes to vocabulary growth (Anglin, 1993) and that vocabulary knowledge contributes to reading comprehension (Stahl & Fairbanks, 1986).

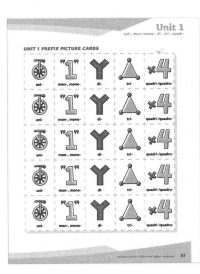

PICTURE CARDS

For each prefix, there is a postage-stamp-size picture icon students can tape to the front or back of their word cards. Make one copy of this page for every five students. Give each student a strip of icons to cut apart and tape to their word cards.

REVIEW GAMES

After every two units, there is a game to play to review and reinforce word learning. These games can be played with words from one or both units, or from other units. For additional challenges, use words from more than two units or add words from other subject areas.

Teaching Tips

▶ Duplicate Unit 1 and staple pages together for each student. Work through the lessons as a group. Encourage students to share their original sentences and drawings. Then have students work on subsequent units independently, spending five or ten minutes sharing their work in small groups.

▶ Post the affixes of the week on chart paper. Have students list words they find in their content-area and independent reading with the target prefix or suffix on the chart. Students can also add these words to their word cards. Encourage students to use these words to make their own crossword puzzles for their classmates to solve.

Review Affixes

English language learners and other students may benefit from reviewing these prefixes, suffixes, and inflected endings, before tackling the more challenging affixes in this book.

Prefix	Meaning	Exemplars
re-	again	rearrange, redo, redraw, rewrite
un-	not	unable, unbelievable, unhappy
un-	opposite of	uncover, unlock, unpack
non-	not	nonfiction, nonstick, nonviolent
dis-	not, opposite	disappear, discontinue, disinfect
dis-	lack of	disbelief, disorganized, disrespect

Suffix	Meaning	Exemplars
-ar, -er, -or	one who	beggar, liar, teacher, writer, actor, editor
-less	without	careless, countless, thoughtless
-ly	(changes an adjective to an adverb)	beautifully, largely, slowly
-er	(comparative: more)	faster, smarter, stronger
-est	(comparative: most)	funniest, nearest, nicest

Review Teaching Tips

▶ Remind students to use context to determine whether words have affixes. Not all words that begin with *re-* begin with a prefix. For example: *redo* means *do again*, but *read* does not mean *advertise again*. Likewise, the letters *-er* at the end of a word are not always a suffix: *older* means *more old*, but *mother* does not mean *more moth*!

▶ Distribute pages from newspapers or magazines, or duplicate pages from reading or content-area texts to pairs of students. Have them circle all the words they find that have a target affix. You may want to include inflected suffixes: *-s, -es, -ed (-d), -ies,* and *–ing.*

▶ Play Prefix-Review Concentration. Duplicate blank game cards (page 56) or use index cards. Write the prefix on one card and a word with the prefix on another card. Make a prefix card for each word used. Play with 16 or more pairs of cards. Place the cards facedown in a 4 x 4 or larger array. The first player turns over two cards. If the cards show a prefix and a word using that prefix, players tell what the prefix means and what the word means. If correct, the player keeps the cards. Then the next player takes a turn. Play until all cards have been matched.

Note: italicized words are additional examples of words with the target affix.

UNIT	AFFIX	MEANING	EXEMPLARS
1 ▶	*uni-* *mon-/mono-*	one	uniform, unilateral, unison, *unicycle** monarchy, monogram, monopoly
	di-	two	dichotomy, digraph, diverge
	tri-	three	triathlete, trilogy, tripod, *tricycle*, *triathlon*
	quadri-/ *quadru*	four	quadriceps, quadruped, quadruple
2 ▶	*-ant*	one who	descendant, immigrant, inhabitant
	-arian/-rian	one who	equestrian, humanitarian, octogenarian
	-eer-/ier	one who	electioneer, financier, qualifier
	-ist	one who practices	accompanist, philanthropist, preservationist
	-wright	one who works with	playwright, shipwright, wheelwright
3 ▶	*equa-/equi-*	same	equator, equinox, equitable, *equal*, *equally*
	magn-	large, great	magnanimous, magnate, magnitude, *magnifying*
	mega-	large	megabyte, megalith, megalopolis, *megaphone*
	micro-	small	microbe, microclimate, microscopic, *microscope*
	multi-	many	multidisciplinary, multifaceted, multitude, *multiply*
4 ▶	*-cule*	small	animalcule, minuscule, molecule
	-let	small	islet, ringlet, rivulet
	-ling	small	fledgling, underling, yearling
	-ose	full of	bellicose, grandiose, verbose
	-ulent	full of	fraudulent, succulent, turbulent
5 ▶	*ad-*	near	adhere, adjacent, adjunct, *adhesive*
	extra-	outside	extracurricular, extraneous, extraterrestrial
	intra-	within	intramural, intrastate, intravenous
	sub-	below	subordinate, substandard, subterranean, *subway*
	trans-	across	transcontinental, transparent, transport

*NOTE: Italicized words are additional examples with the target affixes that appear in the unit but are not in boldface.

UNIT	AFFIX	MEANING	EXEMPLARS
6 ▶	-ary	(noun)	adversary, dispensary, infirmary
	-ery	(noun)	forgery, rookery, stationery
	-ment	(noun)	abridgement, allotment, comportment
	-mony	(noun)	acrimony, matrimony, testimony
	-ory	(noun)	conservatory, dormitory, preparatory
7 ▶	ante-	before	antecedent, antechamber, antedate
	inter-	between	interject, intermediary, intervene
	post-	after	posthumous, postpone, postscript
	pre-	before	precaution, prejudicial, prescience
	retro-	back	retroactive, retrofit, retrospective
8 ▶	-an	(adjective)	authoritarian, herculean, metropolitan
	-ic	(adjective)	characteristic, cinematic, intergalactic
	-ical	(adjective)	economical, mystical, quizzical
	-ish	(adjective)	amateurish, boorish, outlandish
	-ous	(adjective)	autonomous, fatuous, judicious
9 ▶	ab-	away from	abdicate, aberrant, abscond, *abnormal*
	circum-	around	circumference, circumspect, circumvent
	e-	out, away	emigrate, evaporate, evoke, *eject*
	peri-	around	peripatetic, periphery, periscope, *perimeter*
	pro-	forward	proactive, proficient, proliferate, *propeller*
10 ▶	-ade	to make	blockade, masquerade, promenade
	-ate	to make	animate, domesticate, exhilarate, *invigorate*
	-en	to make	embolden, enlighten, hearten
	-fy	to make	exemplify, rectify, solidify, *unify*
	-ize	to make	acclimatize, digitize, popularize

Name _____ Date _____

Hidden Prefixes: Numbers

One or more prefixes are hiding in the clues. Look for the word parts that are the same in the boldfaced examples.

1. This prefix means *one*. A **uniform** is the same outfit or look for everyone in a group. A chorus sings in **unison**, in one voice. A **unilateral** decision is one that is made by a single party or only one side.

   A prefix that means *one* is: ____ ____ ____– .

2. This prefix also means *one*. The ruler of a **monarchy** is a single individual or family. A **monogram** is design made up of the initials of a name. A **monopoly** is a single business that controls the supply of something.

   Another prefix that means *one* is: ____ ____ ____– or ____ ____ ____ ____–.

3. This prefix means *two*. A **digraph** is when two letters act as one, like *ph* in *phone*. To **diverge** means to go in separate directions. A **dichotomy** is a division into two opposite positions or opinions.

   A prefix that means *two* is: ____ ____– .

4. This prefix means *three*. A **trilogy** has three books. A **triathlete** competes in a triathlon of three sports, usually swimming, running and biking. A **tripod** is a stand or stool with three legs.

   A prefix that means *three* is: ____ ____ ____– .

5. This prefix means *four*. Multiply an object or number by four to **quadruple** it. A **quadruped** is an animal that walks on four feet. Your **quadriceps** is a four-part muscle at the front of the thighs.

   A prefix that means *four* is: ____ ____ ____ ____ ____ ____–
   or ____ ____ ____ ____ ____ ____– .

List the prefixes in alphabetical order across the top row. Then, list the boldfaced words containing that prefix in alphabetical order under that prefix. The first one has been started for you.

di-				
dichotomy				

Name _____ Date _____

Cloze Call

Write the missing prefix to complete the unfinished word in each sentence.

1. The camera was placed on a special _____**pod** to keep it steady for long exposures.

2. Working overtime, Harry made four times, or _____**ple**, his base pay.

3. Throughout the palace you will see the image of the fire-breathing dragon, which is the symbol of the _____**archy**.

4. The kids in my school wear blue and gray _____**forms**, except on Fridays when we can wear what we want.

5. The class worked in teams to find examples of _____**graphs**, such as *phone*, *theory*, and *child*, in their books.

Use an answer from above in a sentence of your own.
Underline the word with the prefix in your sentence.

_____

_____

Draw a picture to illustrate your sentence.

Name _____   Date _____

Prefix Crossword Puzzle

Read the clues. Use the prefixes in the box below to complete the puzzle.

> **PREFIXES** *di-, mon-/mono-, quadri-/quadru-, tri-, uni-*

CLUES

ACROSS

2. The school superintendent made this kind of decision about all student clubs.

3. A lion or elephant is this.

8. Instead of her name, Lisette puts her _____ on all her papers.

9. When a company is this, it can charge any price it wants because there is no competition.

10. Roads do this when they split in two different directions.

DOWN

1. A long bike ride can cause these muscles to ache.

4. Choirs work hard to sing in this way.

5. The _____ between the two political groups suggests they'll never reach an agreement.

6. A three-book series.

7. Kim runs, swims, and bikes— she's this kind of athlete.

> **On the back, choose two or more puzzle answers to use in a single sentence.**

Name _____   Date _____

Word Cards

▸ **Complete the word cards.**

▸ **Cut them out and tape or staple them to index cards.**

▸ **On the back, illustrate one word for each prefix.**

▸ **Add the Prefix Picture Card from your teacher to the front or back of the card.**

PREFIX *uni-*

Means _____

Words I know with *uni-*:

1. *uniform* means _____

2. *unilateral* means _____

3. *unison* means _____

4. Other words I know with *uni-*:

_____

PREFIX *mon-, mono-*

Mean _____

Words I know with *mon-, mono-*:

1. *monarch* means _____

2. *monogram* means _____

3. *monopoly* means _____

4. Other words I know with *mon-, mono-*:

_____

PREFIX *di-*

Means _____

Words I know with *di-*:

1. *dichotomy* means _____

2. *digraph* means _____

3. *diverge* means _____

4. Other words I know with *di-*:

_____

PREFIX *tri-*

Means _____

Words I know with *tri-*:

1. *trialthlete* means _____

2. *trilogy* means _____

3. *tripod* means _____

4. Other words I know with *tri-*:

_____

PREFIX *quadri-/quadru-*

Means _____

Words I know with *quadri-/quadru-*:

1. *quadriceps* means _____

2. *quadruped* means _____

3. *quadrupled* means _____

4. Other words I know with *quadri-/quadru-*:

_____

Name _____ Date _____

Hidden Suffixes: One Who

One or more suffixes are hiding in the clues. Look for the word parts that are the same in the boldfaced examples.

1. This suffix means *one who*. An **inhabitant** is one who inhabits or lives in a place. An **immigrant** is one who immigrates or comes from another place to live in a new place. A **descendant** is one who descends from others in a family.

   A suffix that means *one who* is: –____ ____ ____ .

2. These suffixes also mean *one who*. A **qualifier** is someone who qualifies or has the skills to advance to the next round. An **electioneer** is a person who works during an election to help a candidate get elected. A **financier** is someone who works with finances or money.

   Suffixes that mean *one who* are: –____ ____ ____ and –____ ____ ____.

3. This is another suffix that means *one who*. An **octogenarian** is someone who is between 80 and 89 years of age. A **humanitarian** is someone who works for the good of all people. An **equestrian** is someone who rides horses.

   Suffixes that mean *one who* are : –____ ____ ____ ____ ____ and –____ ____ ____ ____.

4. This suffix means *one who practices or does*. A **preservationist** is one who does work to preserve or save. An **accompanist** accompanies, or plays the piano for, singers or dancers. A **philanthropist** does good works to benefit others.

   A suffix that means *one who practices* is : –____ ____ ____ .

5. This suffix means *one who works on or with*. A **playwright** writes plays. A **shipwright** builds or works with ships. A **wheelwright** builds or repairs wheels.

   A suffix that means *one who works on or with* is : –____ ____ ____ ____ ____ ____.

List the suffixes in alphabetical order across the top row. Then, list the boldfaced words containing that suffix in alphabetical order under that suffix. The first one has been started for you.

-ant				
descendant				

Name _____   Date _____

Cloze Call

Write the missing suffix to complete the unfinished word in each sentence.

1. The museum hired additional **preservation**_____s to repair tapestries damaged in the flood.

2. The Wild West show's stagecoach wheels were made by a **wheel**_____ who used tools from that era.

3. A **financ**_____ helped the partners raise money for their new business.

4. My great-grandparents were Polish **immigr**_____s who came to America in 1925.

5. The champion **equest**_____ easily cleared the fences on her two-year-old horse, Trigger.

Use an answer from above in a sentence of your own.
Underline the word with the suffix in your sentence.

_____

_____

Draw a picture to illustrate your sentence.

Name _____   Date _____

Suffix Crossword Puzzle

Read the clues. Use the suffixes in the box below to complete the puzzle.

SUFFIXES -ant, -arian/-rian, -ier/-eer,-ist, -wright

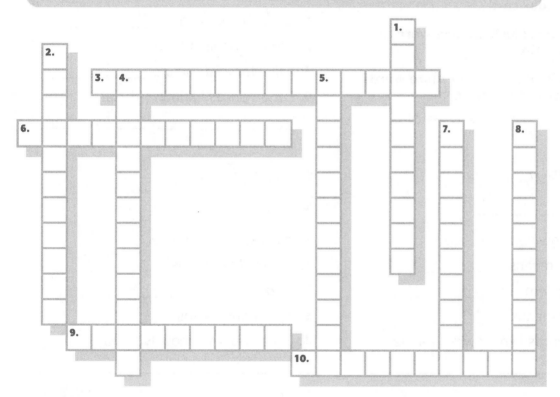

On the back, choose two or more puzzle answers to use in a single sentence.

CLUES

ACROSS

3. This person might donate a lot of money to a hospital or museum.

6. This person plays the piano at a dance class.

9. This runner won his heat. Now he is a _____ in the quarterfinal round.

10. A resident.

DOWN

1. From your great-great-grandmother, you are this.

2. This worker might hand out flyers that tell why you should vote for his candidate.

4. Someone who donates a lot of time and effort to helping people

5. My 84-year-old grandmother is this.

7. William Shakespeare may be the most famous one.

8. She designs and builds yachts.

Name _____   Date _____

Word Cards

▸ **Complete the word cards.**

▸ **Cut them out and tape or staple them to index cards.**

▸ **On the back, illustrate one word for each suffix.**

▸ **Draw a picture of one or more words on the back of the card.**

SUFFIX -ist

Means _____

Words I know with -ist:

1. *accompanist* means _____
2. *preservationist* means _____
3. *philanthropist* means _____
4. Other words I know with -ist:

_____

SUFFIXES -eer, -ier

Mean _____

Words I know with -eer, -ier:

1. *financier* means _____
2. *electioneer* means _____
3. *qualifier* means _____
4. Other words I know with -eer, -ier:

_____

SUFFIX -ant

Means _____

Words I know with -ant:

1. *descendant* means _____
2. *inhabitant* means _____
3. *immigrant* means _____
4. Other words I know with -ant:

_____

SUFFIX -wright

Means _____

Words I know with -wright:

1. *shipwright* means _____
2. *playwright* means _____
3. *wheelwright* means _____
4. Other words I know with -wright:

_____

SUFFIXES -arian, -rian

Mean _____

Words I know with -arian, -rian:

1. *octogenarian* means _____
2. *humanitarian* means _____
3. *equestrian* means _____
4. Other words I know with -arian, -rian:

_____

Review Game 1: Word Hunt

SKILL Identify words with prefixes and suffixes in context.
NUMBER OF PLAYERS Pairs
OBJECT OF THE GAME To find words with affixes in print materials

MAKE THE GAME CARDS

1. Duplicate the blank game cards (page 56) and give two to each student. (You can also use index cards.) Have students select a prefix and a suffix from Units 1 and 2 and write them on their game cards. Instruct students to write their initials in the corner of each card.

2. Collect the prefix cards and suffix cards separately. Mix up each group. Give pairs of students two cards from each group.

PLAY THE GAME

1. Have pairs talk about their affixes. Encourage them to make their own list of words with each affix as they discuss the kinds of reading materials (newspapers, magazines, nonfiction, fiction, encyclopedias) where they might find words with the affixes.

2. In the classroom or school library, direct each team of pairs to quietly look for their affixes in different print materials. When they find a word with the affix, have the team record the following information on the card: the title of the book or article, its author, the page and sentence where the word appears.

3. The first team to find all their affixes in context scores 10 points. Then, they separate and help others find theirs. The next team to find all their affixes scores 9 points. Then those students separate, helping still other teams. Play continues until all affixes have been found.

4. Collect all the completed cards. Read one context sentence aloud. Have students (other than the pair who found the sentence) guess the source of the sentence: encyclopedia, newspaper, magazine, novel, mystery, and so on.

NOTE You can play this game with the review affixes (see page 8) and also with other units in this book.

Name _____   Date _____

Hidden Prefixes: Size and Amount

One or more prefixes are hiding in the clues. Look for the word parts that are the same in the boldfaced examples.

1. This prefix means *small.* Use a microscope to examine something extremely small or **microscopic**, such as a **microbe**. A **microclimate** is the climate in a small geographical area or a confined space, such as a terrarium.

A prefix that means *small* is: ____ ____ ____ ____ ____- .

2. This prefix means *large.* If your computer has one **megabyte** of memory, it can store one million bytes. A **megalith** is an enormous standing stone from a prehistoric structure. A **megalopolis** is an area where several large cities and their suburbs are so close it's as if they were one huge city.

A prefix that means *large* is: ____ ____ ____ ____- .

3. This prefix also means *large.* A **magnate** is a wealthy, powerful businessperson. If that person were also very kind and very generous, she would be described as **magnanimous**. The **magnitude** of something is its importance, greatness, or size.

A prefix that also means *large*: ____ ____ ____ ____- .

4. This prefix means *many.* A **multitude** of something is a huge amount or number. A **multidisciplinary** study involves more than one skill or subject. A **multifaceted** gem has many facets or cut surfaces. A multifaceted person has many different talents.

The prefix that means *many* is : ____ ____ ____ ____ ____- .

5. These prefixes mean *same.* The **equator** is an imaginary line around the center of Earth, dividing our planet into equal halves. The **equinox** is one of two yearly crossings of the equator by the sun (March 21 and September 23). During the spring or fall equinox, the number of hours in the day and the night are nearly the same. When you share something equally, you've made an **equitable** division.

The prefixes that mean *same* are : ____ ____ ____ ____- and ____ ____ ____ ____-.

List the prefixes in alphabetical order across the top row. Then, list the boldfaced words containing that prefix in alphabetical order under that prefix. The first one has been started for you.

equa-/equi-				
equator				

Name _____ Date _____

Cloze Call

Write the missing prefix to complete the unfinished word in each sentence.

1. The _____**animous** billionaire donated money to rebuild all the schools damaged in the hurricane.

2. The _____**climate** in the terrarium was a perfect mini rain forest.

3. The social studies, science, and history departments led a _____**disciplinary** study of early settlers to the island.

4. The most _____**able** way to share a sandwich is to for one person to cut it in half and for the other person to pick the half he or she wants.

5. The area comprising Boston, New York, Philadelphia, and Washington, D.C., is often referred to as a _____**lopolis**.

Use an answer from above in a sentence of your own.
Underline the word with the prefix in your sentence.

_____

_____

Draw a picture to illustrate your sentence.

Name _____   Date _____

Prefix Crossword Puzzle

Read the clues. Use the prefixes in the box below to complete the puzzle.

> **PREFIXES** *equa-/equi-, magn-, mega-, micro-, multi-*

CLUES

ACROSS

2. This describes something so small it can't be seen with the naked eye.

5. This imaginary line circles the globe from east to west.

7. The biathlon, triathlon, or decathlon attracts this kind of athlete.

9. Twice a year this occurs, and there is an equal number of daylight and nighttime hours.

10. Some computers have memory calculated in these.

DOWN

1. A virus or bacteria is this.

3. A huge stone, like the ones at Stonehenge in England

4. A _____ of people watched President Obama being sworn into office.

6. An enormously successful and influential businessperson

8. The _____ of destruction in the wake of the tornado was horrifying.

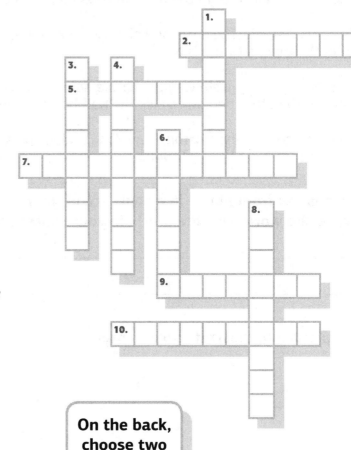

> **On the back, choose two or more puzzle answers to use in a single sentence.**

Name _____   Date _____

Word Cards

▶ **Complete the word cards.**

▶ **Cut them out and tape or staple them to index cards.**

▶ **On the back, illustrate one word for each prefix.**

▶ **Add the Prefix Picture Card from your teacher to the front or back of the card.**

PREFIX micro-

Means _____

Words I know with micro-:

1. microbe means _____

2. microclimate means _____

3. microscopic means _____

4. Other words I know with micro-:

_____

PREFIX mega-

Means _____

Words I know with mega-:

1. megalith means _____

2. megalopolis means _____

3. megabyte means _____

4. Other words I know with mega-:

_____

PREFIXES equa-, equi-

Mean _____

Words I know with equa-, equi-:

1. equator means _____

2. equinox means _____

3. equitable means _____

4. Other words I know with equa-, equi-:

_____

PREFIX magn-

Means _____

Words I know with magn-:

1. magnitude means _____

2. magnanimous means _____

3. magnate means _____

4. Other words I know with magn-:

_____

PREFIX multi-

Means _____

Words I know with multi-:

1. multifaceted means _____

2. multidisciplinary means _____

3. multitude means _____

4. Other words I know with multi-:

_____

Unit 4
-cule, -let, -ling, -ose, -ulent

Name _____   Date _____

Hidden Suffixes: Size and Amount

One or more suffixes are hiding in the clues. Look for the word parts that are the same in the boldfaced examples.

1. This suffix means *small*. A **yearling** is an animal, such as a calf or deer, between one and two years old. A **fledgling** is bird with new feathers needed for flight. It may also refer to a young or inexperienced person. An **underling** is someone who works under another person and is of less importance at that job.

A suffix that means *small* is: –____ ____ ____ ____.

2. This suffix also means *small*. An **islet** is a small island. A **ringlet** is a small curl of hair. A **rivulet** is a small stream or river.

Another suffix that means *small* is: –____ ____ ____.

3. This suffix means *very small*. Something that is **minuscule** is extremely small. A **molecule** is a particle of one or more atoms. You'll need a microscope to see an **animalcule**, a microscopic organism, such as an amoeba.

A suffix that means *very small* is: –____ ____ ____ ____.

4. This suffix means *full of*. Something that is juicy, or full of juice, and delicious is **succulent**. A succulent is also a kind of plant with thick, fleshy leaves and stems that can store water. Something that is **turbulent** is full of violent motion, unstable, or chaotic. That which is **fraudulent** is false, full of fraud, and aiming to deceive.

A suffix that means *full of* is: –____ ____ ____ ____ ____.

5. This suffix also means *full of*. People who are **verbose** are talkative, long-winded, and use too many words to express themselves. Someone who is **bellicose** is aggressive and quick to fight. Something **grandiose** is full of grandeur to the point of being showy and ostentatious.

Another suffix that means *full of* is : –____ ____ ____.

List the suffixes in alphabetical order across the top row. Then, list the boldfaced words containing that suffix in alphabetical order under that suffix. The first one has been started for you.

-cule				
animalcule				

Name _____ Date _____

Cloze Call

Write the missing suffix to complete the unfinished word in each sentence.

1. The **fraud**_____ scheme robbed hundreds of people of their life savings.

2. We knew it was going to be a long meeting because the chairperson is so **verb**_____.

3. We each had a chance to look at the tiny **animal**_____ through a microscope.

4. The general's **under**_____s were proud to serve, even if the general did not know their names.

5. While white water rafting on the river, we passed many **rivu**_____s that were too narrow for our craft.

Use an answer from above in a sentence of your own.
Underline the word with the suffix in your sentence.

_____

_____

Draw a picture to illustrate your sentence.

Name _____ Date _____

Suffix Crossword Puzzle

Read the clues. Use the suffixes in the box below to complete the puzzle.

> **SUFFIXES** *-cule, -let, -ling, -ose, -ulent*

CLUES

ACROSS

2. A single unit of one or more atoms

5. You do not want an airplane ride to be this!

9. You do not want a raise at work to be this size!

10. This baby bird is ready to learn to fly.

DOWN

1. We rested on the _____ in the stream before paddling home.

3. Quick to anger, ready to fight

4. Showy and ostentatious

6. A curl of hair

7. A cactus is this kind of plant because it can store water.

8. The doe stayed close to her _____.

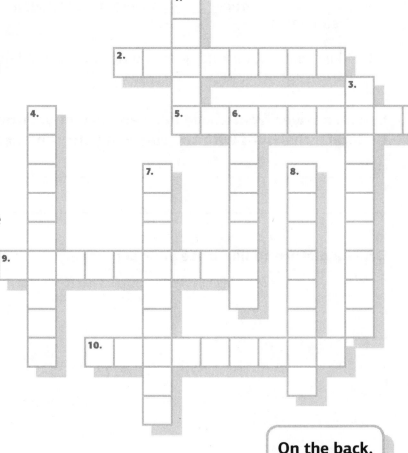

On the back, choose two or more puzzle answers to use in a single sentence.

Name _____   Date _____

Word Cards

▸ **Complete the word cards.**

▸ **Cut them out and tape or staple them to index cards.**

▸ **On the back, illustrate one word for each suffix.**

▸ **Draw a picture of one or more words on the back of the card.**

SUFFIX *-ulent*

Means _____

Words I know with *-ulent:*

1. *turbulent* means _____
2. *fraudulent* means _____
3. *succulent* means _____
4. Other words I know with *-ulent:*

_____

SUFFIX *-ose*

Means _____

Words I know with *-ose:*

1. *verbose* means _____
2. *bellicose* means _____
3. *grandiose* means _____
4. Other words I know with *-ose:*

_____

SUFFIX *-cule*

Means _____

Words I know with *-cule:*

1. *minuscule* means _____
2. *molecule* means _____
3. *animalcule* means _____
4. Other words I know with *-cule:*

_____

SUFFIX *-ling*

Means _____

Words I know with *-ling:*

1. *yearling* means _____
2. *fledgling* means _____
3. *underling* means _____
4. Other words I know with *-ling:*

_____

SUFFIX *-let*

Means _____

Words I know with *-let:*

1. *rivulet* means _____
2. *islet* means _____
3. *ringlet* means _____
4. Other words I know with *-let:*

_____

Prefix and Suffix Password

SKILL Identify prefix or suffix from exemplars
NUMBER OF PLAYERS Pairs
OBJECT OF THE GAME To name the prefix or suffix when given a list of exemplars
ADDITIONAL MATERIALS Minute timer

MAKE THE GAME CARDS

1. Duplicate the blank game cards (page 56) and give six to each student. (You can also use index cards.) Have students select three prefixes and three suffixes from Units 3 and 4. Then have them write the affixes (one per card) at the top of each card and list three exemplars for each prefix and suffix.

2. Collect the cards from all students and mix them up. Give each player six cards facedown in a pile.

PLAY THE GAME

1. Player 1 gives the word clues. Player 2 guesses the prefix or suffix.

2. Player 1 starts the timer and reads the list of words on the first card. Then Player 2 names the prefix or suffix and its meaning. If Player 2 is correct, he or she gets the card. If Player 2 is incorrect, Player 1 keeps the card. Player 2 can choose not to guess and say, "Pass." Player 1 then places the "pass" card at the bottom of his or her pile and goes to the next card.

3. Play continues for one minute, until the timer runs out.

4. Players switch roles and now use the other pile of word cards. Player 2 starts the timer and reads the list of words on the first card to Player 1. This time, if Player 1 names the prefix or suffix and its meaning correctly, he or she keeps that card. If Player 1 answers incorrectly, Player 2 keeps the card. Player 1 can also use the "pass" option.

5. Again, play continues for one minute, until the timer runs out.

6. The player with the most cards at the end wins.

Name _____ Date _____

Hidden Prefixes: Location

One or more prefixes are hiding in the clues. Look for the word parts that are the same in the boldfaced examples.

1. This prefix means *near*. Things that are **adjacent** are connected and share a border or edge. To **adhere** means to stick firmly to, or strictly obey. An **adjunct** is a person who works closely as an assistant to someone in a superior position.

    A prefix that means *near* is: ____ ____– .

2. This prefix means *across*. A trip from one side of the continent to the other is **transcontinental**. To **transport** is to carry from one place to another. Something that is **transparent** is easy to see through or across.

    A prefix that means *across* is: ____ ____ ____ ____ ____–.

3. This prefix means *below*. **Subterranean** means under or below ground. A **subordinate** is someone who works under or for someone else. **Substandard** means poor quality or below acceptable standards.

    A prefix that means *below* is: ____ ____ ____– .

4. This prefix means *outside*. Something **extraterrestrial** is from beyond the Earth and its atmosphere. **Extracurricular** activities are things you do outside of the regular school day. Something that is **extraneous** is outside or beyond what is needed, or not relevant.

    The prefix that means *outside* is: ____ ____ ____ ____ ____– .

5. This prefix means *within*. **Intramural** sports are games played by teams in the same school. **Intravenous** medicines are put directly into the veins. Travel that is **intrastate** is a trip taken within one state. (Note: *inter*state means between two or more states.)

    The prefix that means *within* is: ____ ____ ____ ____ ____– .

List the prefixes in alphabetical order across the top row. Then, list the boldfaced words containing that prefix in alphabetical order under that prefix. The first one has been started for you.

ad-				
adhere				

Name _____ Date _____

Cloze Call

Write the missing prefix to complete the unfinished word in each sentence.

1. The playground is _____*jacent* to the ballfield, so parents sitting on the benches can watch both.

2. The "red eye" is an overnight _____*continental* flight that arrives at 6AM.

3. The house won't be ready as promised because some of the work was _____*standard* and had to be done over.

4. Glee Club, Debate Team, and Future Scientists are the _____*curricular* clubs that meet after school on Wednesdays.

5. The doctors gave him _____*venous* medication so it would start to work faster.

Use an answer from above in a sentence of your own.
Underline the word with the prefix in your sentence.

_____

_____

Draw a picture to illustrate your sentence.

Name _____ Date _____

Prefix Crossword Puzzle

Read the clues. Use the prefixes in the box below to complete the puzzle.

> **PREFIXES** *ad-, extra-, intra-, sub-, trans-*

CLUES

ACROSS

3. Clear glass is this.

5. A nurse's aide is this and reports to the head nurse.

7. All my relatives live in Ohio. We are an _____ family.

10. Conveniently, the classroom is _____ to the library.

DOWN

1. A game played between teams from the same school.

2. To carry

4. The subway is this kind of train.

6. The editor took out these unnecessary details.

8. The _____ teacher assisted the professor during final exams.

9. "No ad-libbing! Just _____ to the script!"

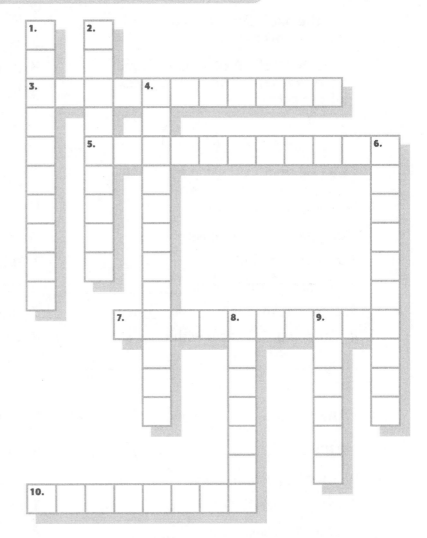

> **On the back, choose two or more puzzle answers to use in a single sentence.**

Unit 5

ad-, extra-, intra-, sub-, trans-

Name _____   Date _____

Word Cards

▸ **Complete the word cards.**

▸ **Cut them out and tape or staple them to index cards.**

▸ **On the back, illustrate one word for each prefix.**

▸ **Add the Prefix Picture Card from your teacher to the front or back of the card.**

PREFIX *ad-*

Means _____

Words I know with *ad-*:

1. *adjacent* means _____

2. *adhere* means _____

3. *adjunct* means _____

4. Other words I know with *ad-*:

_____

PREFIX *trans-*

Means _____

Words I know with *trans-*:

1. *transparent* means _____

2. *transcontinental* means _____

3. *transport* means _____

4. Other words I know with *trans-*:

_____

PREFIX *sub-*

Means _____

Words I know with *sub-*:

1. *substandard* means _____

2. *subordinate* means _____

3. *subterranean* means _____

4. Other words I know with *sub-*:

_____

PREFIX *extra-*

Means _____

Words I know with *extra-*:

1. *extraterrestrial* means _____

2. *extracurricular* means _____

3. *extraneous* means _____

4. Other words I know with *extra-*:

_____

PREFIX *intra-*

Means _____

Words I know with *intra-*:

1. *intramural* means _____

2. *intravenous* means _____

3. *intrastate* means _____

4. Other words I know with *intra-*:

_____

Name _____   Date _____

Hidden Suffixes: Nouns

One or more suffixes are hiding in the clues. Look for the word parts that are the same in the boldfaced examples.

1. This suffix usually turns a word into a *noun*—a person, place, thing or state of being. If you had a fistfight with an **adversary**, an enemy or competitor, you might end up injured and ill. An **infirmary** is where you go to see a nurse or doctor when you are infirm, or sick. The place where the medicine you might need is given out, or dispensed, is a **dispensary**.

   A *noun*-forming suffix is: –____ ____ ____.

2. This is also a *noun*-forming suffix. A school that prepares you for college is a **preparatory**. A school that focuses on art and music is a **conservatory**. A conservatory is also a glass-walled room for growing, displaying, and conserving plants. If you go to a boarding school, you might sleep in a **dormitory**, a large room or building with beds for many.

   A *noun*-forming suffix is: –____ ____ ____.

3. Here is another *noun*-building suffix. A **testimony** is a sworn statement of truth, given by a witness in court. If the court case is bitter or hostile, it may be filled with **acrimony**. If the case is about a divorce, it will end the marriage, which is the state of **matrimony**.

   This *noun*-building suffix is: –____ ____ ____ ____.

4. This suffix also turns a verb into a *noun*. An **abridgement** is something that has been abridged, or cut short. An **allotment** is the portion allotted to someone, or for some purpose. **Comportment** is how a person behaves; it shows attitude, posture, and manners.

   Another *noun*-forming suffix is: –____ ____ ____ ____.

5. This *noun*-building suffix forms a place or thing. A **rookery** is the place where animals that live in colonies, such as penguins, breed. Very nice paper for writing letters is called **stationery**. If you forge something, you make an illegal copy, a **forgery**.

   Another *noun*-forming suffix is: –____ ____ ____.

List the prefixes in alphabetical order across the top row. Then, list the boldfaced words containing that prefix in alphabetical order under that prefix. The first one has been started for you.

-ary				
adversary				

Name _____   Date _____

Cloze Call

Write the missing suffix to complete the unfinished word in each sentence.

1. In the ring, the boxer faced each **advers**_____ like a roaring tiger, but outside the ring he was known for being gentle and kind.

2. To improve our **comport**_____, we call each other "Miss" or "Mister" and practice walking with books balanced on our heads.

3. The **acri**_____ between the two sides escalated into an all-out war.

4. My grandmother bought me some beautiful, monogrammed **station**_____ for writing important letters.

5. The largest collection of rare orchids grow in the rain forest **conserv**_____ at the botanical gardens.

Use an answer from above in a sentence of your own.
Underline the word with the suffix in your sentence.

_____

_____

Draw a picture to illustrate your sentence.

Name _____   Date _____

Suffix Crossword Puzzle

Read the clues. Use the suffixes in the box below to complete the puzzle.

> **SUFFIXES** -ary, -ery, -ment, -mony, -ory

CLUES

ACROSS

1. The state of being married
5. The school nurse works here.
8. That's not my signature – it's a _____!
9. A witness gives this in a court of law
10. A school that gets you ready for college

DOWN

2. The _____ of his book was 100 pages shorter than the original.
3. A place where medicine is given out
4. Your share is this.
6. Penguins build nests in this place.
7. Students who live at school sleep in this place.

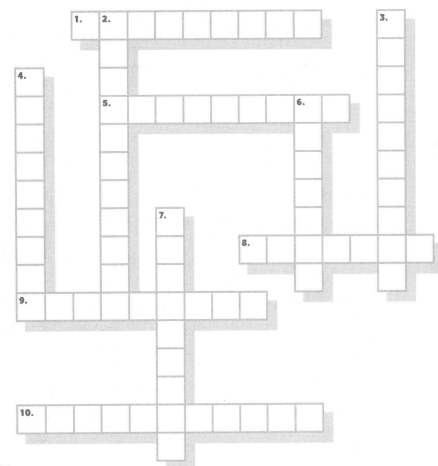

> **On the back, choose two or more puzzle answers to use in a single sentence.**

Name _____   Date _____

Word Cards

▸ **Complete the word cards.**

▸ **Cut them out and tape or staple them to index cards.**

▸ **On the back, illustrate one word for each suffix.**

▸ **Draw a picture of one or more words on the back of the card.**

SUFFIX *-ary*

Means _____

Words I know with *-ary:*

1. *infirmary* means _____

2. *dispensary* means _____

3. *adversary* means _____

4. Other words I know with *-ary:*

_____

SUFFIX *-ory*

Means _____

Words I know with *-ory:*

1. *preparatory* means _____

2. *conservatory* means _____

3. *dormitory* means _____

4. Other words I know with *-ory:*

_____

SUFFIX *-mony*

Means _____

Words I know with *-mony:*

1. *testimony* means _____

2. *acrimony* means _____

3. *matrimony* means _____

4. Other words I know with *-mony:*

_____

SUFFIX *-ment*

Means _____

Words I know with *-ment:*

1. *allotment* means _____

2. *comportment* means _____

3. *abridgement* means _____

4. Other words I know with *-ment:*

_____

SUFFIX *-ery*

Means _____

Words I know with *-ery:*

1. *forgery* means _____

2. *stationery* means _____

3. *rookery* means _____

4. Other words I know with *-ery:*

_____

Review Game 3: Prefix and Suffix Baseball

SKILL Identify prefixes and suffixes, give examples and sentences.
NUMBER OF PLAYERS Whole class
OBJECT OF THE GAME To name a word with a specific prefix or suffix and use that word correctly in a sentence.

MAKE THE GAME CARDS

1. Duplicate the blank game cards (page 56) and give four to each student. Have each student select two Word Cards from Unit 5 and two from Unit 6. Instruct them to write the affix, its definition, and four examples on their four blank game cards.

2. Collect all the word cards, mix them up, and place them facedown in a pile.

PLAY THE GAME

1. The class plays as a single team, with the teacher as pitcher. Designate corners of the room as home plate, first base, second base, and third base. The pitcher sits in the middle of the room.

2. Students line up along the side of the room by home plate.

3. The first batter steps up to the plate.

4. The pitcher turns over the first card and reads the affix and its definition aloud. The batter must name a word with the affix and use it correctly in a sentence to "make a hit" and get on base. If the batter cannot both name the word and use it in a sentence, the student scores an out. Players advance from base to base as batters correctly name example words and use them in sentences. Each player who returns to home plate scores a point for the class. Play until all students have had a turn at bat.

5. Record the date and number of runs and outs. Play again later in the week and compare.

Name _____ Date _____

Hidden Prefixes: Time

One or more prefixes are hiding in the clues. Look for the word parts that are the same in the boldfaced examples.

1. This prefix means *back*. **Retroactive** means to go back and apply something to time in the past and up to the present. If it is March, and your parents raise your allowance retroactively to January, you will get more money for March and the added amount for January and February, too. When you **retrofit** a machine, you go back and add or change parts that were not there originally. A **retrospective** is a look backward at the past, particularly at a person's life work or career.

   A prefix that means *back* is: ____ ____ ____ ____ ____- .

2. This prefix means *after*. To **postpone** an appointment is to do it after or later than originally planned. A **postscript** at the bottom of a letter is a short message added after the signature. A **posthumous** prize is awarded after the winner has died.

   A prefix that means *after* is: ____ ____ ____ ____- .

3. This prefix means *before*. Your grandparents are your **antecedents**—they were born before you. An **antechamber** is a small room before or leading to a larger room. To **antedate** means to put an earlier date on something.

   A prefix that means *before* is: ____ ____ ____ ____- .

4. This prefix also means *before*. Putting on a bike helmet before riding is a **precaution**, a safety measure taken before an activity. A **prejudicial** opinion can be hurtful and harmful, and comes before getting to know a new person, or learning the facts of a legal case. Someone with **prescience** knows what will happen before it occurs.

   Another prefix that means *before* is: ____ ____ ____- .

5. This prefix means *between*. If you try to stop two people from fighting by getting between them, you **intervene**. An **intermediary** is someone who carries messages between two parties or tries to solve a dispute for others. To **interject** means to say or add something to a conversation in a way that interrupts the discussion.

   A prefix that means *between* is: ____ ____ ____ ____ ____- .

List the prefixes in alphabetical order across the top row. Then, list the boldfaced words containing that prefix in alphabetical order under that prefix. The first one has been started for you.

ante-				
antecedents				

Name _____ Date _____

Cloze Call

Write the missing prefix to complete the unfinished word in each sentence.

1. The ambassador acted as an _____**mediary** between the rebels and the government.

2. The actors and singers waited in the _____**chamber** before they were called in to the conference room to audition.

3. The reduced club dues were made _____**active** to last year because so many longtime members complained about having paid the higher rates for so long.

4. The Nobel Peace Prize was given _____**humously**, six months after the winner had died.

5. The jury was not permitted to read the newspaper or watch the news because it could have been _____**judicial** to the case they were judging.

Use an answer from above in a sentence of your own.
Underline the word with the prefix in your sentence.

_____

_____

Draw a picture to illustrate your sentence.

Name _____ Date _____

Prefix Crossword Puzzle

Read the clues. Use the prefixes in the box below to complete the puzzle.

> **PREFIXES** *ante-, inter-, pre-, post-, retro-*

CLUES

ACROSS

1. The museum had this kind of an exhibition, showcasing all of the artist's lifework to date.

4. Knowledge of what will happen in the future

6. Her _____ came to America on the Mayflower.

8. The meeting had to be _____ because half the group had the flu.

9. A parent might do this when you fight with your brother.

10. Modify or install new parts that were not there originally

DOWN

2. To interrupt

3. Helmets and kneepads are these.

5. To change the date to an earlier one

7. Add this to a letter below your signature.

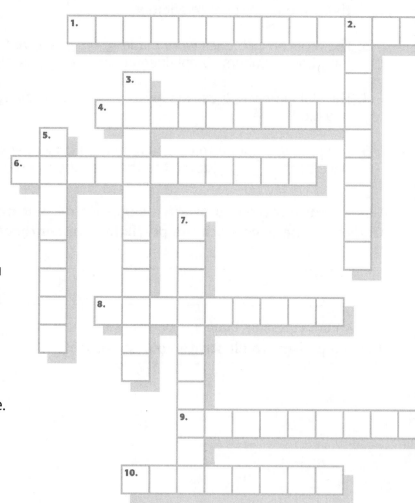

> **On the back, choose two or more puzzle answers to use in a single sentence.**

Name _____   Date _____

Word Cards

▸ **Complete the word cards.**

▸ **Cut them out and tape or staple them to index cards.**

▸ **On the back, illustrate one word for each prefix.**

▸ **Add the Prefix Picture Card from your teacher to the front or back of the card.**

PREFIX *retro-*

Means _____

Words I know with *retro-*:

1. *retroactive* means _____
2. *retrofit* means _____
3. *retrospective* means _____
4. Other words I know with *retro-*:

_____

PREFIX *post-*

Means _____

Words I know with *post-*:

1. *postpone* means _____
2. *postscript* means _____
3. *posthumous* means _____
4. Other words I know with *post-*:

_____

PREFIX *ante-*

Means _____

Words I know with *ante-*:

1. *antecedent* means _____
2. *antechamber* means _____
3. *antedate* means _____
4. Other words I know with *ante-*:

_____

PREFIX *pre-*

Means _____

Words I know with *pre-*:

1. *precaution* means _____
2. *prejudicial* means _____
3. *prescience* means _____
4. Other words I know with *pre-*:

_____

PREFIX *inter-*

Means _____

Words I know with *inter-*:

1. *intervene* means _____
2. *interject* means _____
3. *intermediary* means _____
4. Other words I know with *inter-*:

_____

Name _____ Date _____

Hidden Suffixes: Adjectives

One or more suffixes are hiding in the clues. Look for the word parts that are the same in the boldfaced examples.

1. This *adjective*-forming suffix turns nouns and verbs into describing words. A **metropolitan** area is a big city, or is near or part of a city. An **authoritarian** ruler is a rigid, demanding, and very strict leader. A **herculean** task requires tremendous physical or mental strength or courage, a job Hercules himself might find difficult.

An adjective suffix is: –____ ____.

2. This is also an *adjective*-forming suffix. A typical trait that describes a person or story character is a **characteristic** trait. A movie is a **cinematic** version of a story. If that story is about travel between galaxies, it's an **intergalactic** story.

Another adjective suffix is: –____ ____.

3. This is another *adjective*-forming suffix. When you buy a large size bottle of vitamins, it is usually cheaper and more **economical** than buying smaller bottles. If the label on the vitamins promises to cure everything and bring world peace, those pills better have **mystical** or supernatural magical powers. If you read that label with a critical eye, you would be **quizzical**—both curious and surprised—that a vitamin could bring about world peace.

This adjective suffix is: –____ ____ ____ ____.

4. This suffix also turns a noun into an *adjective*. An **amateurish** performance is a poor one, done by an amateur, not a professional. If the performer acts like a bad sport, or like a boor, when you don't applaud wildly, his behavior is **boorish**. And if he gives a poor performance, but acts like he just won an Academy Award, his behavior is **outlandish**— extremely unusual, strange, and just plain bizarre!

An adjective suffix is: –____ ____ ____.

5. This is still another *adjective*-forming suffix. A smart, fair choice (one that a judge might make) is a **judicious** choice. But a foolish, idiotic choice is a **fatuous** one. Whatever the decision, if you've made it independently, all by yourself, you've made an **autonomous** choice.

Another adjective-forming suffix is: –____ ____ ____.

List the suffixes in alphabetical order across the top row. Then, list the boldfaced words containing that suffix in alphabetical order under that suffix. The first one has been started for you.

-an			
authoritarian			

Name _____   Date _____

Cloze Call

Write the missing suffix to complete the unfinished word in each sentence.

1. Advances in solar-powered space travel have made **intergalact**_____ exploration beyond our solar system possible.

2. They chose to stay at the least expensive, most **economic**_____ hotel near the water park.

3. The student council wishes it were an **autonom**_____ group, able to make decisions without the approval of a teacher advisor or the principal.

4. The production was so **amateur**_____, the performers sounded as though they had never had a singing lesson.

5. Although the commander was an **authoritari**_____ leader when in uniform, he was a relaxed, team player when not on duty.

Use an answer from above in a sentence of your own.
Underline the word with the suffix in your sentence.

_____

_____

Draw a picture to illustrate your sentence.

Name _____ Date _____

Suffix Crossword Puzzle

Read the clues. Use the suffixes in the box below to complete the puzzle.

> **SUFFIXES** -an, -ic, -ical, -ish, -ous

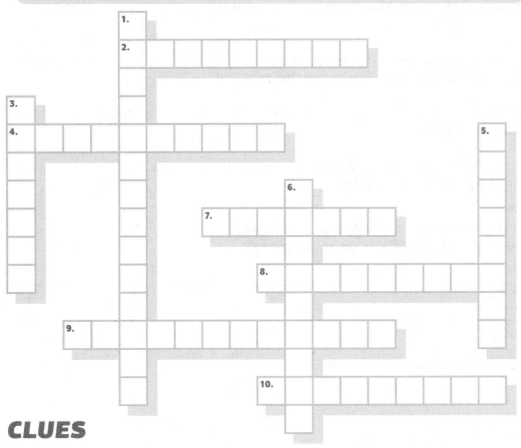

On the back, choose two or more puzzle answers to use in a single sentence.

CLUES

ACROSS

2. A _____ effort was needed to clean up after the hurricane.

4. Shockingly bizarre behavior

7. A silly and foolish decision is this.

8. Like a movie

9. They lived in the Boston _____ area.

10. Surprisingly curious

DOWN

1. Typical of someone

3. Behaving in a rude, obnoxious manner

5. Powers a wizard might have

6. A carefully considered, fair decision or choice is this.

Name _____   Date _____

Word Cards

▸ **Complete the word cards.**

▸ **Cut them out and tape or staple them to index cards.**

▸ **On the back, illustrate one word for each suffix.**

▸ **Draw a picture of one or more words on the back of the card.**

SUFFIX -an

Means _____

Words I know with -an:

1. authoritarian means _____

2. herculean means _____

3. metropolitan means _____

4. Other words I know with -an:

_____

SUFFIX -ic

Means _____

Words I know with -ic:

1. characteristic means _____

2. cinematic means _____

3. intergalactic means _____

4. Other words I know with -ic:

_____

SUFFIX -ish

Means _____

Words I know with -ish:

1. amateurish means _____

2. boorish means _____

3. outlandish means _____

4. Other words I know with -ish:

_____

SUFFIX -ical

Means _____

Words I know with -ical:

1. economical means _____

2. quizzical means _____

3. mystical means _____

4. Other words I know with -ical:

_____

SUFFIX -ous

Means _____

Words I know with -ous:

1. autonomous means _____

2. fatuous means _____

3. judicious means _____

4. Other words I know with -ous:

_____

Review Game 4: Cloze Concentration

SKILL Use words with affixes to complete sentences.
NUMBER OF PLAYERS Pairs
OBJECT OF THE GAME Match words to cloze sentences.

MAKE THE GAME CARDS

1. Duplicate four pages of blank game cards (page 56) for each pair of players.

2. Give each player two pages of blank game cards. Have students select a total of nine words from Units 7 and 8 and write them on the left side. Then have them write a cloze sentence for each word on the right. Where the target word would appear in the sentence, have students draw a box, as shown below:

POSTPONE	We had to [ ] the game because of rain.

Each student should also have one set of blank word cards. Have them write "Wild Card" on these cards.

3. Before cutting apart the cards, students should review each other's words and sentences to be sure they are correct. Have students cut apart the cards. For durability, tape game cards to index cards.

4. Each pair of students should have a total of 40 game cards: 18 sets of word and cloze sentence cards, plus four Wild Cards. Place each pair's game cards in an envelope. Have students write their initials in the top right corner of the envelope. Collect the envelopes.

PLAY THE GAME

1. Randomly distribute the envelopes, making sure that no pair gets its own set of game cards.

2. Players mix up the cards and place them facedown in a 5 x 8 array.

3. Play Concentration. The first player turns over two cards. If the cards show a word and a cloze sentence that the word completes, the player then identifies the prefix or suffix and its meaning. If correct, the player keeps the cards. If the player turns over a Wild Card, he or she writes a word with an affix or composes a sentence to make a pair. If the player does this correctly, the player keeps the cards. Then the next player takes a turn.

4. If the cards don't match, or the player incorrectly defines the affix and/or its meaning, the cards are turned facedown for the second player's turn.

5. The player with the most cards at the end wins.

Name _____   Date _____

Hidden Prefixes: Direction

One or more prefixes are hiding in the clues. Look for the word parts that are the same in the boldfaced examples.

1. This prefix means *away from*. To **abdicate** means to give up or resign from a position or responsibility. To **abscond** is to run away, escape, or make off with something, usually stolen valuables. Both behaviors, abdicating and absconding can be **aberrant**—unusual and abnormal, veering away from the norm.

   A prefix that means *away from* is: ____ ____–.

2. This prefix means *out* or *away*. To **emigrate** means to move away from the country where you were born. People who emigrate might feel that the way of life they knew has **evaporated**—vanished like water changing from liquid to vapor. Folk songs from the old country may **evoke**—bring out, bring to mind, or call forth—memories of the way things used to be.

   A prefix that means *out* or *away*: ____–.

3. This prefix means *around*. The perimeter of a shape is the outer edge. When you are on the edge around a playing field you are on the **periphery**. A **periscope** is an instrument that lets you see all around. A **peripatetic** teacher is a teacher who travels around from school to school.

   A prefix that means *around* is: ____ ____ ____ ____–.

4. This prefix also means *around*. The **circumference** the measurement of the outside of a circle. When you try to **circumvent** rules, you try to get around or avoid the rules. And if you are **circumspect**, meaning careful and cautious, you might succeed.

   Another prefix that means *around* is: ____ ____ ____ ____ ____ ____–.

5. This prefix means *forward*. When you are **proactive**, you work ahead to solve problems. If you are talented and make progress by performing well, you are **proficient**. Something that grows, advances, or multiplies rapidly **proliferates**. A *propeller* moves an airplane forward.

   A prefix that means *forward* is: ____ ____ ____–.

List the prefixes in alphabetical order across the top row. Then, list the boldfaced words containing that prefix in alphabetical order under that prefix. The first one has been started for you.

ab-				
abdicate				

Name _____   Date _____

Cloze Call

Write the missing prefix to complete the unfinished word in each sentence.

1. The _____**ference** of the tricycle's front wheel is larger than the two back wheels.

2. Heat from the sun causes the water to _____**vaporate**, leaving the sea salt behind.

3. Fears that nuclear weapons might _____**liferate** led the United Nations to ban the sale of such weapons.

4. When our nation was young, _____**patetic** teachers and peddlers traveled from village to village.

5. The _____**errant** behavior of the animals led the zookeepers to suspect that the new feed might be contaminated.

Use an answer from above in a sentence of your own.
Underline the word with the prefix in your sentence.

_____

_____

Draw a picture to illustrate your sentence.

Name _____   Date _____

Prefix Crossword Puzzle

Read the clues. Use the prefixes in the box below to complete the puzzle.

> **PREFIXES** *ab-, circum-, e-, peri-, pro-*

CLUES

ACROSS

2. Careful and cautious

4. The king had to _____ his throne to marry the commoner he loved.

6. Very good at something

7. Thieves do this with stolen goods.

9. The outer edge

10. To move from your country to live in a new place

DOWN

1. Working to predict and solve a problem is _____.

3. Submarines use this instrument to see above the surface.

5. If you try to go around the rules, you do this.

8. Bring to mind

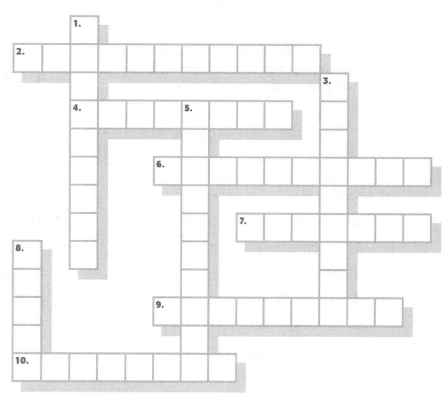

> **On the back, choose two or more puzzle answers to use in a single sentence.**

Name _____   Date _____

Word Cards

- ▶ **Complete the word cards.**

- ▶ **Cut them out and tape or staple them to index cards.**

- ▶ **On the back, illustrate one word for each prefix.**

- ▶ **Add the Prefix Picture Card from your teacher to the front or back of the card.**

PREFIX *ab-*

Means _____

Words I know with *ab-*:

1. *abdicate* means _____

2. *aberrant* means _____

3. *abscond* means _____

4. Other words I know with *ab-*:

_____

PREFIX *circum-*

Means _____

Words I know with *circum-*:

1. *circumference* means _____

2. *circumspect* means _____

3. *circumvent* means _____

4. Other words I know with *circum-*:

_____

PREFIX *e-*

Means _____

Words I know with *e-*:

1. *emigrate* means _____

2. *evaporate* means _____

3. *evoke* means _____

4. Other words I know with *e-*:

_____

PREFIX *peri-*

Means _____

Words I know with *peri-*:

1. *peripatetic* means _____

2. *periphery* means _____

3. *periscope* means _____

4. Other words I know with *peri-*:

_____

PREFIX *pro-*

Means _____

Words I know with *pro-*:

1. *proactive* means _____

2. *proficient* means _____

3. *proliferate* means _____

4. Other words I know with *pro-*:

_____

Name _____   Date _____

Hidden Suffixes: "To Make"

One or more suffixes are hiding in the clues. Look for the word parts that are the same in the boldfaced examples.

1. This suffix means *to make*. To **animate** means to liven up, bring to life, or make active. And if you feel especially animated, you might also feel **exhilarated**, excited, invigorated, and very happy to be alive. Although we want our pets to be happy, they also need to behave. To **domesticate** means to tame or make behave.

   A suffix that means *to make* is: –____ ____ ____ .

2. This is another verb suffix that means *to make*. If you **masquerade** as a VIP, you disguise yourself and make yourself out to be someone very important. And if you try to get into a party uninvited, guards might **blockade**, or block your entrance. If that happens, you should probably give up and **promenade**, walk or stroll home.

   A suffix that means *to make* is: –____ ____ ____ .

3. This suffix also means *to make*. A photograph or TV signal is **digitized**, made or changed into digital form, then reformatted so you can see it on your TV or computer screen. Inventors try to **popularize** their gadgets, hoping to make them popular and get rich. When people get used to having gadgets to do things, or when they adapt to new environments, they become **acclimatized** to those things.

   This suffix meaning *to make* is: –____ ____ ____ .

4. Here's another suffix that means *to make*. Make yourself bold, brave, **emboldened**, and say, "I love you." You'll feel **heartened** when your sweetheart says, "I love you, too." A wise and philosophical friend might try to **enlighten** you by saying, "One day you will find that special someone to love."

   A suffix that means *to make* is: –____ ____ .

5. This is yet another suffix that means *to make*. To make or set a good example is to **exemplify** the right or correct way. To correct a mistake is to **rectify** an error. To strengthen and unify a lead is to **solidify** a winning position.

   A suffix that means *to make* is: –____ ____ .

List the suffixes in alphabetical order across the top row. Then, list the boldfaced words containing that suffix in alphabetical order under that suffix. The first one has been started for you.

-ade				
blockade				

Name _____ Date _____

Cloze Call

Write the missing suffix to complete the unfinished word in each sentence.

1. Paintings on cave walls prove that early man **domestic_____d** dogs for protection and companionship.

2. In small towns, the only evening activity is to **promen_____** around the village square.

3. The researchers needed weeks to **acclimat_____** themselves to the thin air of the their mountaintop observation post.

4. When the cat was at the vet's, the mice were **embold_____ed** to scurry around during the day.

5. Pages from the manual **exempli_____** how a correctly erected tent should look.

Use an answer from above in a sentence of your own.
Underline the word with the suffix in your sentence.

_____

_____

Draw a picture to illustrate your sentence.

Name _____ Date _____

Suffix Crossword Puzzle

Read the clues. Use the suffixes in the box below to complete the puzzle.

> **SUFFIXES** *-ade, -ate, -en, -fy, -ize*

CLUES

ACROSS

5. To give hope or courage

9. What cartoon illustrators do to make drawings come to life

10. By the end, the detective will _____ us as to who did it.

DOWN

1. Enemy ships _____ the port so supplies could not reach the people.

2. To make fashionable or trendy

3. Winning the gold medal _____ her whole team.

4. To disguise

6. To correct a mistake

7. The team that wins this game will _____ a number one rating.

8. A converter box will do this to television signals.

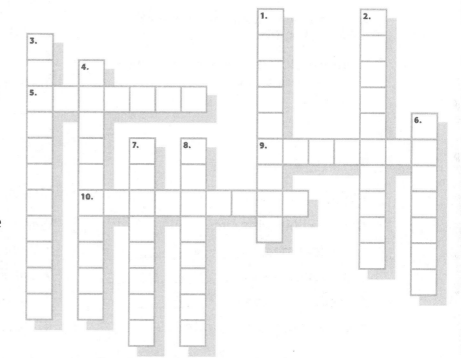

> **On the back, choose two or more puzzle answers to use in a single sentence.**

Name _____   Date _____

Word Cards

▸ **Complete the word cards.**

▸ **Cut them out and tape or staple them to index cards.**

▸ **On the back, illustrate one word for each suffix.**

▸ **Draw a picture of one or more words on the back of the card.**

SUFFIX *-ade*

Means _____

Words I know with *-ade:*

1. *blockade* means _____

2. *masquerade* means _____

3. *promenade* means _____

4. Other words I know with *-ade:*

_____

SUFFIX *-ate*

Means _____

Words I know with *-ate:*

1. *animate* means _____

2. *domesticate* means _____

3. *exhilarate* means _____

4. Other words I know with *-ate:*

_____

SUFFIX *-en*

Means _____

Words I know with *-en:*

1. *embolden* means _____

2. *enlighten* means _____

3. *hearten* means _____

4. Other words I know with *-en:*

_____

SUFFIX *-fy*

Means _____

Words I know with *-fy:*

1. *exemplify* means _____

2. *rectify* means _____

3. *solidify* means _____

4. Other words I know with *-fy:*

_____

SUFFIX *-ize*

Means _____

Words I know with *-ize:*

1. *acclimatize* means _____

2. *digitize* means _____

3. *popularize* means _____

4. Other words I know with *-ize:*

_____

Review Game 3: A Picture Is Worth . . .

SKILL Write sentences using words with affixes.
NUMBER OF PLAYERS Whole class
OBJECT OF THE GAME To write sentences for student-drawn illustrations
MATERIALS Drawing and writing materials

MAKE THE GAME CARDS

Give each student three blank game cards (page 56) or index cards, and drawing paper.

MAKE THE GAME ART

1. Students select three words to illustrate from Units 9 and 10. They write their chosen words on individual game cards (page 56) or index cards, and use drawing paper to illustrate each word. On the back of the game or index card, students write a sentence, or caption, to go with their picture. Tell students they will score points for each word used correctly in their sentences.

2. Students select their favorite artwork for display and put away (out of view) the game card that goes with it.

3. Collect the favorite words, number them, and tack or tape them around the room in numerical order.

PLAY THE GAME

1. Down the left side of a piece of writing paper, students list the numbers of displayed drawings.

2. Let students walk around the room looking at the pictures. Next to each number on their paper, students write the word they think is being illustrated, and a sentence to go with the picture. Students skip their own word.

3. When students have their words and sentences, have the class share their sentences for each. Students score 1 point for correctly identifying the word illustrated, and 1 point for each word used correctly in their sentence.

4. After all students have shared their sentences, the artist reads his or her original caption for the picture. Sentences that use all the same words (not necessarily in the same order) as the artist's, score an extra 5 points.

Game Cards

See directions for review games on pages 19, 28, 37, 46, and 55.

UNIT 1 PREFIX PICTURE CARDS

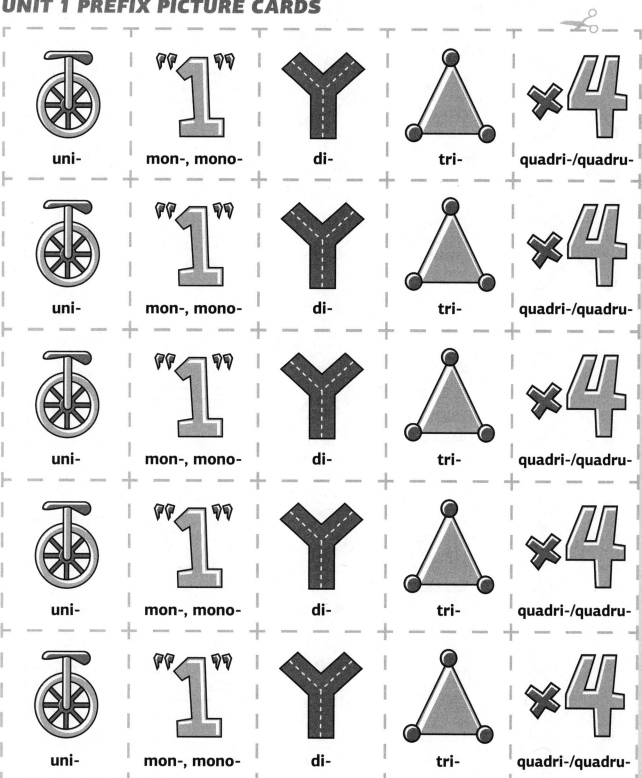

uni-	mon-, mono-	di-	tri-	quadri-/quadru-
uni-	mon-, mono-	di-	tri-	quadri-/quadru-
uni-	mon-, mono-	di-	tri-	quadri-/quadru-
uni-	mon-, mono-	di-	tri-	quadri-/quadru-
uni-	mon-, mono-	di-	tri-	quadri-/quadru-

UNIT 3 PREFIX PICTURE CARDS

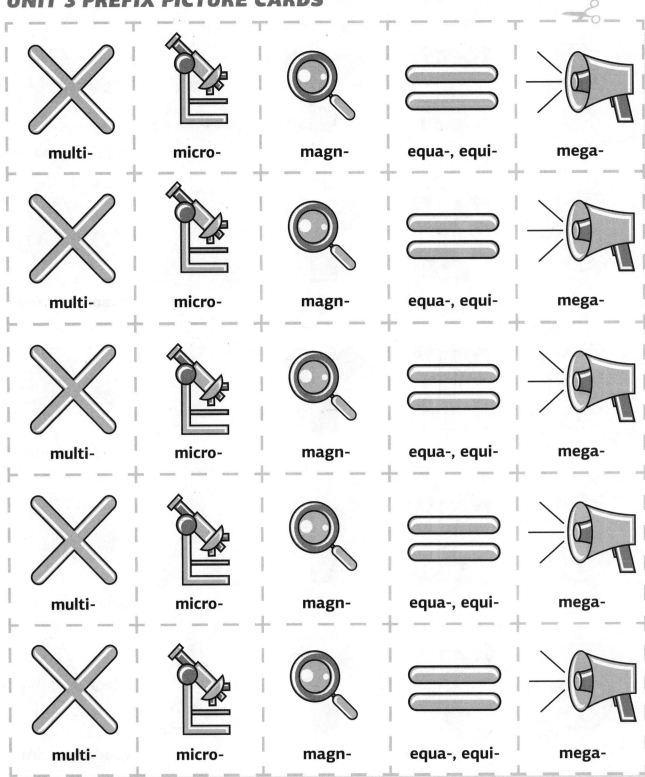

multi-	micro-	magn-	equa-, equi-	mega-
multi-	micro-	magn-	equa-, equi-	mega-
multi-	micro-	magn-	equa-, equi-	mega-
multi-	micro-	magn-	equa-, equi-	mega-
multi-	micro-	magn-	equa-, equi-	mega-

UNIT 5 PREFIX PICTURE CARDS

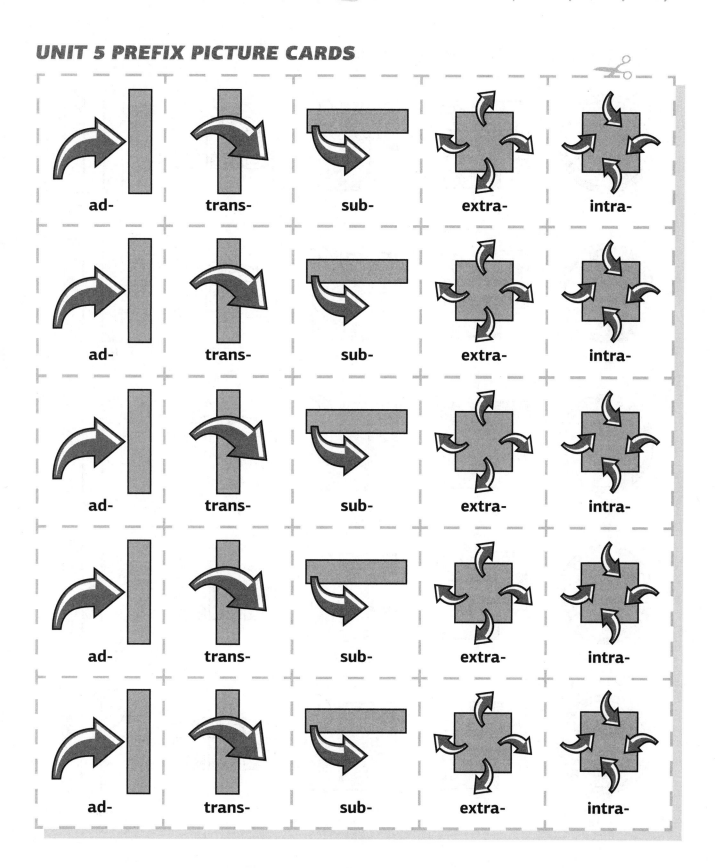

Unit 7

ante-, inter-, post-, pre-, retro-

UNIT 7 PREFIX PICTURE CARDS

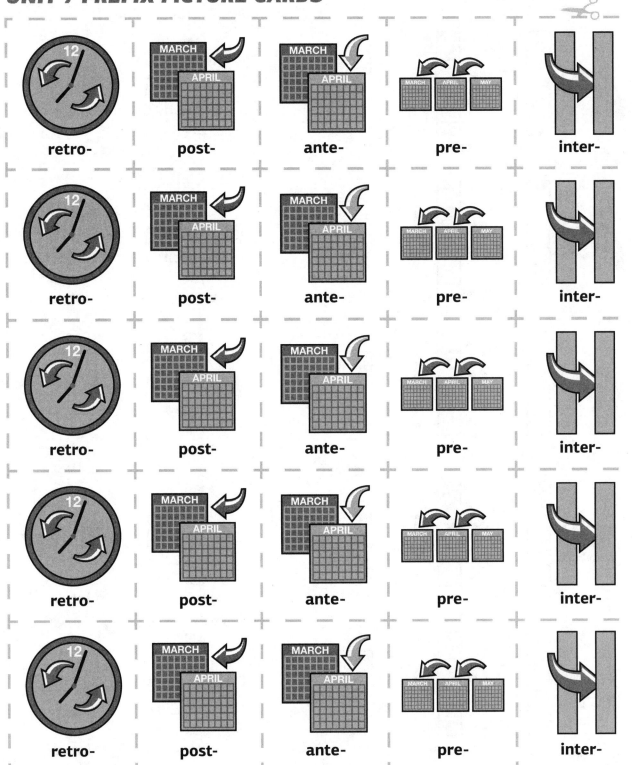

UNIT 9 PREFIX PICTURE CARDS

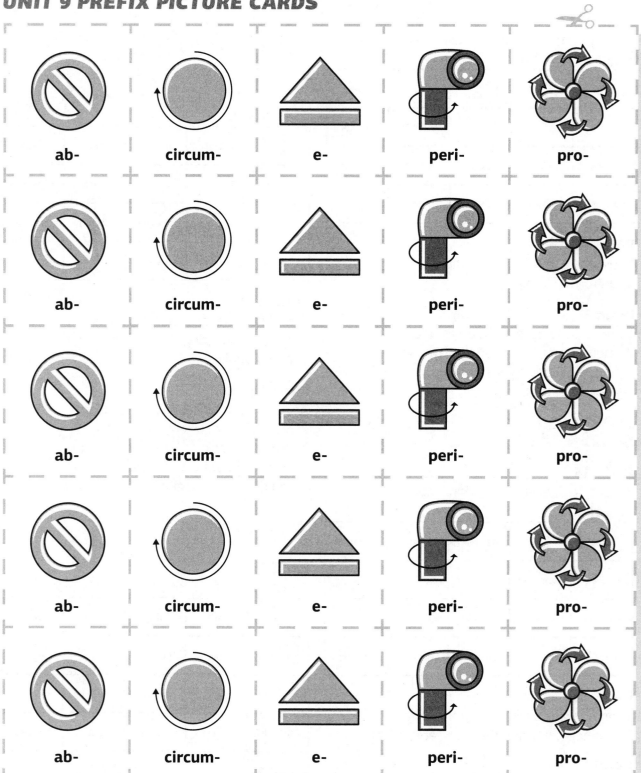

ab-	circum-	e-	peri-	pro-
ab-	circum-	e-	peri-	pro-
ab-	circum-	e-	peri-	pro-
ab-	circum-	e-	peri-	pro-
ab-	circum-	e-	peri-	pro-

Answer Key

Unit 1

PAGE 11
1. uni-, 2. mon-/mono-, 3. di- 4. tri-,
5. quadri-/quadru-

di-	mon-/mono-	quadri-/quadru-	tri-	uni-
dichotomy	monarchy	quadriceps	triathlete	uniform
digraph	monogram	quadruped	trilogy	unilateral
diverge	monopoly	quadruple	tripod	unison

PAGE 12
1. tripod, 2. quadruple, 3. monarchy,
4. uniforms, 5. digraphs

PAGE 13
Across: 2. unilateral, 3. quadruped,
8. monogram, 9. monopoly, 10. diverge
Down: 1. quadriceps, 4. unison, 5. dichotomy,
6. trilogy, 7. triathlete

Unit 2

PAGE 15
1. -ant, 2. -eer/-ier, 3. -arian/-rian, 4. -ist,
5. -wright

-ant	-arian/-rian	-eer /-ier	-ist	-wright
descendant	equestrian	electioneer	accompanist	playwright
immigrant	humanitarian	financier	philanthropist	shipwright
inhabitant	octogenarian	qualifier	preservationist	wheelwright

PAGE 16
1. preservationists, 2. wheelwright,
3. financier, 4. immigrants, 5. equestrian

PAGE 17
Across: 3. philanthropist, 6. accompanist,
9. qualifier, 10. inhabitant
Down: 1. descendant, 2. electioneer,

4. humanitarian, 5. octogenarian,
7. playwright, 8. shipwright

Unit 3

PAGE 20
1. micro-, 2. mega-, 3. magn-, 4. multi-,
5. equa-/equi-

equa-/equi-	magn-	mega-	micro-	multi-
equator	magnanimous	megabyte	microbe	multidisciplinary
equitable	magnate	megalith	microclimate	multifaceted
equinox	magnitude	megalopolis	microscopic	multitude

PAGE 21
1. magnanimous, 2. microclimate,
3. multidisciplinary, 4. equitable,
5. megalopolis

PAGE 22
Across: 2. microscopic, 5. equator,
7. multifaceted, 9. equinox,
10. megabytes
Down: 1. microbe, 3. megalith
4. multitude, 6. magnate, 8. magnitude

Unit 4

PAGE 24
1. -ling, 2. -let, 3. -cule, 4. -ulent, 5. -ose

-cule	-let	-ling	-ose	-ulent
animalcule	islet	fledgling	bellicose	fraudulent
minuscule	ringlet	underling	grandiose	turbulent
molecule	rivulet	yearling	verbose	succulent

PAGE 25
1. fraudulent, 2. verbose, 3. animalcule,
4. underlings, 5. rivulets